Beneath the Light

ALSO BY LAURA LEWIS-WATERS

Bathroom Prisoners

Beneath the Light

Laura Lewis-Waters

QUERENCIA

Querencia Press, LLC
Chicago, Illinois

QUERENCIA PRESS

LIBRARY OF CONGRESS CATALOGING-IN-PUBLICATION DATA

ISBN 978 1 959118 12 1

www.querenciapress.com

First Published in 2023

Querencia Press, LLC
Chicago IL

Printed & Bound in the United States of America

For my mum, all the birth trauma mums, and everyone on the journey of motherhood

Also for Fallon

CONTENTS

Preface

September 2020.
We'd been trying for a baby for years, we'd lost a baby, we'd carried a baby through Covid lockdown, and here I finally was about to have a baby. I'm not sure if anything truly prepares us for childbirth that first time, and certainly a combination of lockdown and my mental health preventing me from reading anything following my miscarriage didn't help, but I still like to think I went into it with an open mind. On my midwife's recommendation I made a birth plan, but let's face it, they really shouldn't be called that. Nothing went to plan, and when I came out of hospital, it was with pain and trauma that I wasn't expecting.

Beneath the Light is a journey, actually two. The first is a journey to the hospital, surgery and the aftermath of PTSD and CBT. It's an acknowledgement of what went wrong. The second is the very long, very slow journey to recovery and the hopeful message that time is a great healer. It's processing the anger, the guilt, the hurt, the happy tears too, and realising that there is hope that a day will come when you don't think about it as much. Within that is also an acknowledgment of the struggles that all new parents face, and, hopefully, a warm embrace and reminder that we are not alone.

I watched the edges
fade inwards
toward the bright light

I may not have died
but this is still life after death
—*how shall I choose to live it?*

September: trauma

The way things started on a mild evening in mid-September

At my mother's. The family dog's last hours. And everyone was sad, so sad. We had a takeaway. What else was there to do? We sat and laughed. We sat and cried. We sat and slowly said our goodbyes. We went home. We went to bed.

Have you ever heard that saying *one in one out*?

I fought sleep. Waited for the night-time kicks. My eyes closed. For a while I dozed. My mother messaged. The dog passed away. I went downstairs. Sat alone in the dark. Gone midnight. I started to wonder. Had there been any kicks? Started to tell myself there hadn't. Started preparing. Got myself ready to go and get checked.

It's always best to go and get checked.

It was dark but still warm. We drove with my almost finished packed bags. Everything's always *almost* with me. We drove through the early hours. To the hospital. It was quiet. It was dark. But triage was hot. I sweated with fear. The machine detected movement. I fell asleep. And I felt guilty for that. Then the doctor came. Told me I wasn't going home.

I said goodbye to my husband. I was all alone. It was dark. A woman had fainted. I was scared to be induced. I was excited to meet the baby. I lay on the bed. I didn't get changed. All of a sudden I was cold. I waited. I tried to sleep. I was scared.

Birth Plan:

- A water birth would be nice/ calming lights to ease the baby into a lilac tinted world/ maybe some soft music, ready to roll over fresh skin, pool around us as we float together.
- We'll be in the Birth Centre/ relaxed, no doctors/ but not far away, just in case
- A bit of gas and air, when the time is right/ a dizzying weightlessness as supple bones swim to life.
- My husband's hand/ on the edge of the pool/ steady, strong/ a lighthouse to draw us back to shore.
- A midwife to smile at me/ warmth/ to tell me I'm doing a good job.
- When the baby is here: delayed cord clamping/ the chance to swim the joyful waves of each other's newness.
- Vitamin K injection

Birth Preferences:

Things don't always go to plan; I know that. But:

- To be listened to [doesn't seem too much to ask]/ be believed when I say I am in pain [maybe be offered more than Paracetamol]/ I know it's been a rough year, but an apology when it becomes known that Paracetamol got me to 10 cm and beyond.
- Intervention [when it was promised the 1st time, 2nd time, 3rd time]/ a little confidence.
- Be told when to stop pushing/ alarm bells for everyone but me/ supple bones tangled.
- My husband's hand/ on the edge of the bed/ steady, strong/ ready to pull us both to safety.
- A midwife to smile at me/ warmth/ to tell me I'm doing a good job/ be present in the room [especially when the doctor is looking away].
- When the baby is here: to hold them/ hold them for more than seconds/ breathe in the joyful scents of each other's newness/ feel soft skin on mine.
- Stay conscious [not see the room swim with darkness, flood with doctors, yellow forms]
- To see life/ not death/ a single, bright light above/ bleeding out/ beckoned towards the rocks.
- Practise breathing exercises/ in out/ in/ out/ without thinking each would be my last.
- Did anyone give the Vitamin K injection?

Legacy

We have a history of quick labour
I proudly beamed at the midwife
as I was rushed down to delivery—
I would make my mother proud
my grandmother proud, I would
continue their legacy, pain free.

I felt the need to push before
I'd seen the light of the incubator
the bed I would give birth on
and I felt my mother push
my grandmother push, I felt
their strength, their power in me.

I knew I would give birth alone
he was moving too quickly
and I felt my own quick birth
my mother's quick birth, my son's—
limbs tangle and become stuck
I pushed, pushed, strength leaving me.

Then I was no longer alone
and too many hours had passed
and their strength, their speed, their
power failed. I felt my mother's distress
my grandmother's distress, the doctors'
distress, as life began to fade within me.

I think the worst part
the absolute
gut wrenching
heart wrenching
soul wrenching
heartrending
agonising
gut wrenching
heart breaking
family breaking
soul destroying
body collapsing
mind deteriorating
excruciating
just plain terrifying
part

is that in the darkness
when I told myself,

this is the moment
to find something to live for,

I found nothing.

Thoughts from the darkness:

Am I still alive?
It's so cold
so this is how women died in childbirth in the 'old days'?
My legs are shaking
I need Edward to turn me into a vampire
still shaking—what if I get a cramp?
I just had a baby
relax: the baby is in good hands
is this really happening to me?
My husband and mother will do a good job
I have accepted it
he will have a good life
now's the time; find something to fight for
I'm okay with dying
why can't I think of anything?
My legs are shaking.

I'm so cold.

Motherbird

The first time I saw
I flew into the room
like a little bird
too frail for even
your fragile mouth
opening and closing
as my heart sped up;
my breathing slowed
green and red wires ran
over my body
like long thin worms
my veins my lifeblood
pulsed to touch you
but my wings were clipped
my lips chapped
and I shook my head
closed my eyes
the biggest regret
my little life will know.

I did not suffer trauma
because my expectations
pool
dim lights
calm music
were not met.

I suffered trauma
because I watched the
edges
fade inwards toward the
bright light
above me while I
stilled
withered
disappeared

Pros and Cons of Birth Trauma

Pros	Cons
<ul><li>Being brought tea and toast to my bed</li><li>My husband feeding me cottage pie over the baby's head</li><li>Breastfeeding pain drowned at the bottom of a medicinal cocktail</li><li>Not being able to change the baby</li><li>Not having to drive</li><li>Having help with everything that needs doing</li></ul>	<ul><li>Cold tea and toast because the doctors are coming</li><li>Losing parts of myself (physical parts too)</li><li>Not being able to sit down/ stand up/ walk around/ get into bed/ pick up the baby/ look after the baby/ carry the baby/ change the baby</li><li>Not being able to drive</li><li>Not having help because a lady on the ward has COVID</li></ul>

Feeding Schedule: ~~baby's~~ mum's

Breakfast: ~~Toast~~ Thyroxine; metallic taste

Snack (30 minutes later. Exact): Biscuit. Two antibiotics. Laxative.

Snack II (must be two hours later): Iron tablets. Sweat; a hard time on the toilet.

Lunch (and must be two hours again): More red and whites; more hard to sit.

Afternoon snack: For the baby only. Milk and cuddles to make it through.

Dinner: Two more hard-to-swallows. A stab in the abdomen. Laxative.

Midnight: A scent of sleep; perhaps lavender; sat upright in bed.

Things I fear since becoming a mother:

dark rooms/ quiet rooms/ my bedroom/ the bathroom/ the stairs/ going to the dentist/ the hospital/ the shop/ pushing shopping trolleys/ pushing pushchairs/ pushing on the toilet/ pushing myself/ my pelvic floor/ tooth extractions/ speculums/ doctor's hands/ my needle-hole riddled hands/ blood/ bright lights/ the toilet/ falling asleep/ compression stockings/ hospital gowns/ sweat-stained pyjamas/ milk-stained pyjamas/ keeping myself clean/ keeping the baby clean/ washing down below/ shaving/ stitches/ vaginas/ my unshaved legs/ razors/ anything sharp/ wires/ the beep of a vital signs machine/ the colour red/ making it to the toilet/ going to the toilet/ not going to the toilet/ wiping myself after the toilet/ bleeding/ not bleeding/ mirrors/ intimacy/ germs/ COVID/ coughing/ infection/ keeping clean/ having a shower/ sweating/ breathing/ not breathing/ sucking in at the ribs/ rashes/ exercising/ not exercising/ never being able to run again/ picking up my baby/ watching babies being born on TV/ having babies/ not having another baby/ breastfeeding in public/ society.

Societal Delivery Scoring System

Score		0 Points	1 Point	2 Points
A	**Assisted**	Caesarean: is that giving birth?	Spoons and cups to pull them out	**Push push push yourself; it's for the best**
P	**Pain relief**	Epidural; injections of this and that	**Paracetamol, a breath of gas and air**	None; a bit of hypnobirthing
H	**Haemorrhage**	**Class 4: 2500 ml; confused; fading fading fading**	Class 2: 750-1500 ml; BP normal; a little anxious	Doing the shopping the next morning
I	**Infection**	**Sepsis charts; heart rate rising**	A bit of a temperature	Fit and strong; able to look after baby
P	**Photograph**	**Unable to hold/ look after/ see baby**	A few here and there; had better looking days	First moments treasured forever

scores of 0-3: you are adequate, you are strong, you are courageous
scores of 4-6: you are adequate, you are strong, you are courageous
scores of 7-10: you are adequate, you are strong, you are courageous

My mother's trauma

As I became a mother
I inherited my mother's trauma

I'd never quite understood
the dread in dark rooms

unable to close our eyes
in case we never wake

anaphylaxis, haemorrhage
it's all the same really

when we are left to fear
our very last breaths.

Notes for midwife

months after birth, alphabetised

Appetite/ aspirin/ blood test/ blood thinners/ blood toilet/ breathlessness/ belly still big/ bleeding/ colic drops/ cord (black?)/ constant sick/ coccyx pain/ dry skin/ discomfort/ doesn't settle/ dirty nappies/ difficult to sit/ eye (lazy)/ exercise?/ fingers still swollen/ faint on the toilet/ go just inside (vagina)/ heavy dragging feeling/ hard belly/ hearing screen/ hiccoughs/ ill on the toilet/ just inside/ jaundice/ kick belly/ laxatives/ massage scar/ more moles/ MRI/ numb bum/ olive oil/ piles/ pain on right side/ period feeling/ period?/ PTSD/ quick feed/ rash/ sick out of nose/ spots/ stitches (healing?)/ sit upright/ Talipes/ tooth extraction?/ ultrasound/ veins raised/ X-Ray/ wheezy/ white spots/ warm breasts/ yellow discharge/ Zoom appointment?

Appointment

I get behind the wheel
I am able to do that

In. Out. In, out

but I am already speeding
vision edges blurring

inout inout inout

each road sign a warning
white-knuckle steering

inoutinoutinout

pull over get out screaming
more unconscious bleeding

outoutoutoutout

focus on the white lines steadying
they manage to keep on going

in in in and out

I walk into the hospital
I am able to do that.

Sometimes I wonder if an old friend
gave me "something" to spite me
for leaving them behind—
that's the level of thought
my mind can reach on days
I'm not sure I want to be here.

I wasn't destined to be a mum
because even though I am, a mum,
someone somewhere wanted to stop me
red warning signs, red spots, haemorrhage
all of this couldn't happen to one person, right?

Clothes

Sometimes, maybe once a month,
I spare a thought for my clothes
the ones that were cut from me,
discarded whilst I stared helplessly
upwards, the bright light washing us.

Sometimes, I spare a thought for the
searing agony, the cold edge of scissors
as they were ripped wide open and tossed
aside, I wonder if anyone gives them
a second thought like I do now.

Sometimes, I wonder about
the new white nursing bra I should
have been wearing as I fed
my baby for the first time.

Sometimes, the guilt consumes me,
I was not strong enough to sit up
and remove them myself, dignified.
Sometimes, I grieve that they did not
make it, like the part of myself I left behind.

Sometimes, I am grateful, *I am*,
that they were sacrificed, quickly, efficiently
so that I could be saved.

Content note: social media

Just in case
    it helps anyone today—

it looks like
    we've had a good day

and we have.

But, at bedtime
    (during the day too)

I notice how much
    pain I am in

and I am.

Because it's not
    all smiles

it's prolapse symptoms
    coccyx pain

it's mental pain.

It's desperation
    to feel healthy again.

if anyone else is
    going through this

you are not alone.

Mundane

I'd like to say that I can remember the little details—

those little pieces of mundane that sit on peripheries
the unremarkable marks on polystyrene ceiling tiles

I'd like to say I can remember something more than
the crashing waves of pain that wracked my body

as faceless hands pounded on my stomach
and I wished for anesthetic or some other ending

I'd like to say I can remember which shade of cream
the walls were, the angle of the blue leather chair

and the way the light slanted across green speckled
tiles before tenderly touching new black hair

I'd like to say I can remember the soft mottled skin
the weight of creation. And I'd really like to remember

something more than the light.

You might feel a bit of pressure
he waves the forceps around
as easy as that.
I open my mouth wide
but the scream stays silent
buried. I close my eyes
it's better not to see
but darkness is not safe either.
He prods, pokes, pulls
then the tooth is out.
I sink back into the chair
it is over—but suddenly
the room floods with dentists
and there are not enough
cotton pads to stop it.
I bite down and
sicken as the saliva-tainted
blood bursts from the pad.
My blood pools the floor
I am drowning drowning
and I am fading fading
and I look up at the light.

I wake up sweating, shaking
and wonder if I will make
my appointment in the morning.

Return to Work

If I told you
that I wasn't terrified about going back to work
I'd be lying
because when standing up is pain and sitting down is pain
and almost every movement is a fibrous tissue strain
it's not easy
and you don't say anything because you don't want to be a drain
and you try to lock it away, fight battles in your brain
you want to be normal.

If I told you
that I hadn't had an accident on my way to the bathroom
I'd be lying
because sometimes it really can't be avoided
but I won't carry spare clothes, that'd destroy me
I just need more time
meanwhile you're thinking about the baby
and you're wondering if life just may be
what it used to be.

March (after next): healing

I squeeze myself in places I never want to see with everything that I have in the hopes that I can squeeze myself back together in places I don't understand and perhaps if I squeeze hard enough, I will escape the black holes

Hello, my name is Laura

after Molly Brodak

I am a good woman.
The amount of time
I spend worrying
if people will come
to my funeral is insane.
Because either they'll come
or they won't.
I want to be loved
but I no longer know how
not to be seen
as dead behind the eyes
but to be seen.
When I'm not tired
I have love to give
but if I'm not quick enough
it seeps through my tears.

Guilt

after Catherine Bell

A drip of not talking to a
growing bump scared of
what might drip
happen drop / a
drip of guilt, of
stress, of doubt /
a drip of something I'm not sure about / a drip
of not being there after you arrived and of with-
holding that first drop of milk / a drip dripping
from a nappy not changed/ a
blueberry pouch drip
for breakfast / a drip
of washing up,
tidying up and a drip
of picking my
phone up/ a drip
to feed you to sleep drop
and a drop when you're in need drop
/ it's a drip to the dentist
to the hospital
to the shop / a
drip of hot choc-
olate, no, actually
a lot / swimming
lessons with a drip of
porridge on your face
drop/it's drips of TV time
nap time, of sleeping on my
lap time/ drop no time for me
time, time for you time, so sorry
there's no time for the zoo time drip/
it's a drip drip with a relentless grip drop/
it's an acceptance that it's not going to stop.

Bones

After Flora Cruft

The bones of life grow
in even uninhabitable places
like those little green shoots
that spring up wilfully
between dusty dry cracks
on climate change posters.

For years the only spring within me
was an ultrasound probe
as I recoiled further into myself
it echoed emptiness onto the screen
there's nothing wrong doctors said
save for a few cysts.

There was nothing else to do
except to wait and medicate
the date of treatment always looming.
But my baby was too unsettled
no comfort would keep them still
and they floated away from me
on a breeze that swept through the car
carrying them off into a night air
tainted with fish and chips.

So I returned to the dirt
buried my face in the darkness of cracks
searching for hopeful green shoots
to try again.

The Mum's Eatwell Guide
Things I feed myself now I have a toddler

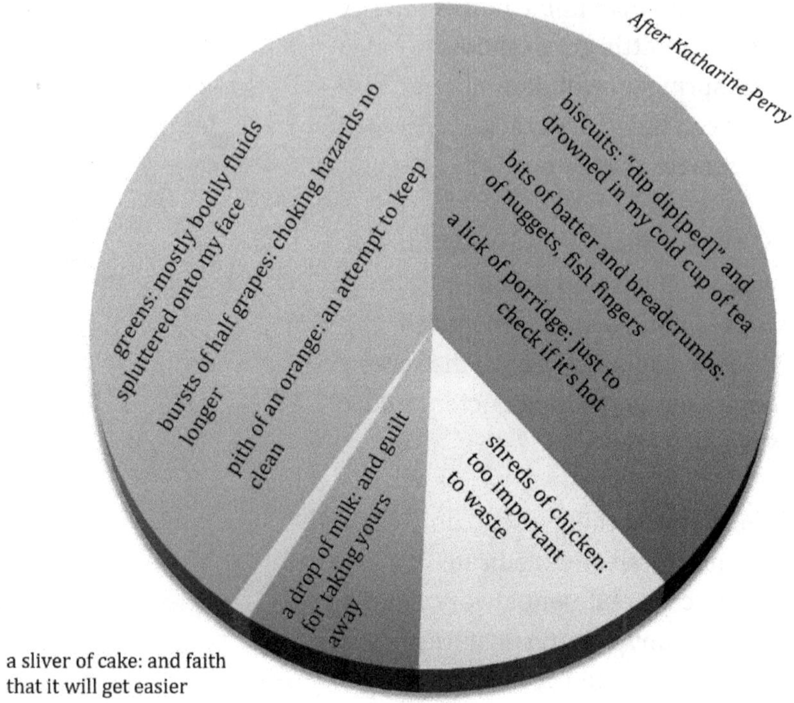

Upgrade storage

My mental capacity has been drained
first the baby-brain, a bit of PTSD

there's the dentist appointments,
blood tests, reviews, and immunisations
them

then the dentist appointments, physio
Obstetric Anal Sphincter Injury, CBT
me

and the snapshots I try to keep of
the way your blue eyes light up

and the space I need for myself.

Birthing Forecast

Mornings, I steadily lose
identity
the way I lost two parts of myself
in that room with the incubator
and absent hands

a physical part—that showed up
as little black holes on future
ultrasounds

and the other, darker part—
the one free to lie under covers
painting constellations on the Artex ceiling
while falling into whatever
Hallmark had to offer.

Now I am good. Moderately good
at scanning the night sky for any gale
at washing myself in the neighbour's
bedroom light, spilling into the street
at 4 am
at sleeping on top of covers
hardened to September-chill

and when I regain myself, I will
become a storm among the stars.

What I fear most about being a mother is not being his world.
What I fear most about being a wife is him wanting something else.
What I fear most about being a daughter is not speaking for myself.
What I fear most about being the eldest sibling is carrying the weight.
What I fear most about being a colleague is not being respected.
What I fear most about being a friend is being forgotten.
What I fear most about being a woman is my female-ness.
What I fear most about the stars is that they will become dull.
What I fear most about being alive is not living enough.
What I fear most about myself is not being enough.

I know I'm not supposed to apologise

but,
I'm sorry I couldn't hold you
lay your soft skin on mine
I'm sorry I had to leave you
for our briefly snatched time
I'm sorry I considered not fighting
lying alone in the dark
I'm sorry I couldn't dress you
a failure from the start
I'm sorry it wasn't beautiful
it wasn't what I'd planned
I'm sorry I wouldn't feed you
be there at your command
I'm sorry that my body
couldn't bend to your will
I'm sorry I couldn't move with you
and had to stay so still
I'm so so sorry my baby
this is not what you deserve
I'm sorry my darling baby
that this happened at your birth.

I'm sorry.
I'm sorry.
I'm sorry.

Some days I **C**an't be **B**othered to **T**ry
Some days I think it **C**an't be **B**ad **T**o
Some days I **C**an **B**elieve it's **T**rue
Some days it just **C**an't **B**reak **T**hrough
Some days it helps to be **C**alm **B**reathe **T**ry
Some days I **C**rack **B**reak **T**ear
Some days I **C**an hope **B**ecause it's **T**here

Cognitive Behavioural Therapy

Do you think he's going to remember?

No.

Do you think he's going to remember?

No.

Do you think he's going to remember?

No.

But I will.

Cognitive Behavioural Therapy II: Intrusive Thoughts

Find something to ground yourself:

His smile.

Find something to ground yourself:

Clap. Clap. Clap.

Find something to ground yourself:

His laugh.

Find something to ground yourself:

Clap. Clap. Clap.

Find something to ground yourself:

His eyes.

Find something to ground yourself:

Clap. Clap. Clap.

Find something to ground yourself:

Sing together.

Find something to ground yourself:

Clap. Clap. Clap.

Find something to ground yourself:

Laugh together.

Find something to ground yourself:

Clap. Clap. Clap.

Medical History

after Nicole Sealey

Patient: Laura Lewis-Waters   Age: 30

I have been pregnant, twice. Carried two, given birth to one. When my son was born, I nearly died. If I can tap my toothbrush just right, I'll admit to having O – C – D. I like to think I caught it from my husband who has Talipes and anxiety. There's always a Sertraline strip on the windowsill. My mother has, mother's father had diabetes. She shares a B12 deficiency with my sister. My other sister has coeliac. My brother is too scared to know his own diagnosis. I don't drink. Don't smoke. I worry. Thyroxine for living. Clomid for hope. My grandmother died of a heart attack. My grandfather disappeared. Great Grandad lost a finger. Uncle Fred died aged 3. And, as I understand it, there can be life after death.

Recipe for trauma healing

I. 5 Tbsp of cottage pie fed lovingly by husband
II. 3 cups of tea and talk with anyone who'll listen
III. 6 tsp of CBT can never really hurt
IV. boil the anger, the doubt; they're better out of the pot
V. 8 pints of water
VI. 1 quart of sun
VII. ¼ tsp of you time

} we're like plants after all

builds into something more

VIII. ½ cup of tears, it won't always be empty
IX. Dashes of sleep here and there remind us how to rest
X. 5 gallons of time. Don't ever underestimate time.

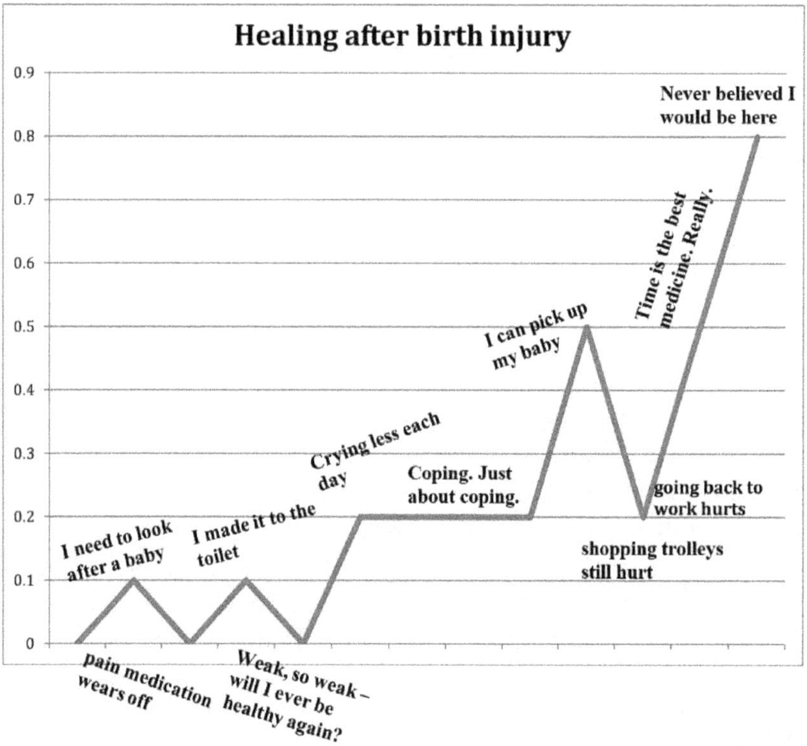

Healing after birth injury
0.9
0.8
0.7
0.6
0.5
0.4
0.3
0.2
0.1
0
Never believed I would be here
Time is the best medicine. Really.
I can pick up my baby
Crying less each day
Coping. Just about coping.
going back to work hurts
shopping trolleys still hurt
I need to look after a baby
I made it to the toilet
pain medication wears off
Weak, so weak – will I ever be healthy again?

Est. 2020

after Kaitlyn Wislang

In the Factory of Motherhood
stamped with Est. 2020 branding
I am dispatched to the under 2's section
where bright-eyed mothers with enthusiasm
in tact encourage their little ones to crawl.
But I don't belong here, I think.
Mine's mobile and halfway up the slide
on double run time while I'm still hoping
for the down time I was promised.
I glance back through the tangle
of mesh web, a hint of envy directed
towards those steaming white mugs
before a muffled laugh bursts stretched
and lopsided from the mirror and I am back
on the belt. I am spun, shook and slid
testing my quality, my strength, my resolve.
Most days I assume I won't make the cut
that I'll be flushed out in a flurry
of dirty nappies and cleaning chemicals,
but I end up right back here, padding
softly behind, half in chase.

And there amongst the soft materials
and components, our love is manufactured
and CE marked with a cacophony of
joyful screams and outstretched arms.

And beneath those large, dim, yellow lights

with my son by my side

I realise

I have never felt more alive

Tips for the soft play slide

I've found,

that if you lean

back

as far as you can

while sitting

place your feet

hip-width

apart

all your weight

on them

lift your hips

ever so slightly

on the bump

then the grimace

is barely

noticeable

Fallon's hands

I lie back on the bed,
feel my legs begin to shake
before I've even dropped my knees,
my hands slick with sweat bear
half-moon nail marks

but Fallon's hands are soft hands

they don't rush or judge
the lack of strength I carry inside,
even when the paper covering beneath
me slips as I shake with silent exertion
and invisible perspiration

Fallon's hands are soft hands

and they won't belittle me
or tire from my asking if I can run
if I'll ever be the same, if I'll
run a cross-country again
because

Fallon's hands are soft hands

and they listen without being asked,
stay late to keep me calm, voices
of reassurance
Fallon's hands always ask how I am:
and they truly mean it too

Fallon's hands are soft hands

and sometimes they grip my own
like when the car park is full and I'm
forty minutes late to be prodded and

probed, and I sob to them
and they give me faith
because

Fallon's hands are soft hands
and they are a little light in the dark.

Haiku for sleep

You lie on my chest
peaceful as the sun rises
a hard night has passed

Things I am grateful for:

The warm incubator light that first held my son/ the rapid response of the doctors who rushed in to help/ the doctor with blonde hair who wore a mask for her asthma/ the doctor with brown hair who spoke in the darkness/ the anaesthetist with the kind face who checked my legs/ the doctor that used my name and asked how I was/ the stitching (I hear it was a really neat job)/ the person with my blood type and a heart much bigger than mine/ the ICU tea and toast/ the lady who dressed me/ the gentle bed bath/ the lady with the bright smile, a beacon in the dark/ the midwife that helped my baby latch on/ the beautiful baby asleep in my arms

Rites

(inspired by the Chinese tale of Li Ji and the Giant Serpent)

They call me *girl-eating serpent*
put me on a mountain-high pedestal

so that they can perform their rituals
in the shadows of the Yung

but I have my own ritual magic
and I tap tap tap my sword

grate it against my teeth
hack at scales

draw the serpent into being
with my tongue,

against my cheek, round
and round and if I do it just right

maybe I too will be able
to have children of my own.

Cold Season

The best thing about having a cough
during my inner winter
is not needing to worry
about getting wet.

Sleepless

I wake to sun
dripping thick honey into the room
and onto our faces
your eyes are heavy-lidded
after Eunice upset you in the night
but we bunkered down
came out the other side in each other's arms.

I watch dust motes swim
let myself go with them, just for a moment,
I feel the warmth of your fingers
reaching out before you latch
I see a perfect curl, a hint of a smile
and I am thankful for that.

General Synopsis 09.19

Waxing crescent. September.
First phase. New moon.
Light breeze. North-westerly.

She didn't see it. She didn't
feel it. But she knew.
That she would regain

her power, her strength.
Her mother knew it.
Her grandmother knew it.

She would comb the night
through her hair and drink
lightly punctured air.

Notes on Previous Publications

Things I fear since becoming a mother featured on BBC Upload Coventry and Warwickshire (radio) and BBC Upload Festival 2022 (video)

Content note: social media featured in Corporeal Lit Mag, Volume 5, September 2022

Medical History in Bathroom Prisoners, Bent Key Publishing, May 2022

Recipe for trauma healing featured in Hope is a Group Project, The Wee Sparrow Press, August 2022

Healing after birth injury featured in Corporeal Lit Mag, Volume 5, September 2022

Rites featured in Li Ji: Courage and the serpent, Free Verse Revolution Arts and Literary Magazine, May 2022 and in their 'Best of' anthology, Truthtellers, January 2023

Recipe for trauma healing was also nominated for the 2022 Pushcart Prize

Acknowledgements

Firstly, thank you to Emily; this wouldn't exist without you. It has been wonderful working with you.

Thank you to the doctors and staff in surgery with me that day at University Hospital Coventry and Warwickshire for bringing me back from the darkness; to Fallon for being much more than a physiotherapist; and to the OASI clinic team.

Thank you to The Mum Poem Press and the members of the Mum Poet Club for the support and confidence and for the inspiration for some of the poems here. Rebecca Green, much gratitude for the workshops and feedback.

Thank you to Rebecca Kenny and Korrin Smith-Whitehouse for all of the poetic opportunities you have so kindly given to me this year. You have inspired and allowed me to grow in confidence.

Thank you to my husband, Shaun, for looking after all of us in the first couple of weeks afterwards; and the rest of the time too. Thank you to family and friends who constantly checked in on me and offered to help.

Finally, thank you to my beautiful son and best friend, William, for being everything I ever dreamt of and more and for making it all worthwhile.

CPSIA information can be obtained
at www.ICGtesting.com
Printed in the USA
BVHW051916170223
658757BV00006B/88

9 781959 118121